Recipes to Share
SLOW COOKER

Publications International, Ltd.
Favorite Brand Name Recipes at www.fbnr.com

Preparation/Cooking Times: Preparation times are based on the approximate amount of time required to assemble the recipe before cooking, baking, chilling or serving. These times include preparation steps such as measuring, chopping and mixing. The fact that some preparations and cooking can be done simultaneously is taken into account. Preparation of optional ingredients and serving suggestions is not included.

Table of
CONTENTS

Crowd-Pleasing APPETIZERS

Asian Barbecue Skewers

2 pounds boneless skinless chicken thighs
½ cup soy sauce
⅓ cup packed brown sugar
2 tablespoons sesame oil
3 cloves garlic, minced
½ cup thinly sliced green onions (optional)
1 tablespoon toasted sesame seeds

1. Cut each thigh into 4 pieces about 1½ inches thick. Thread chicken onto 7-inch wooden skewers, folding thinner pieces, if necessary. Place skewers in 6-quart slow cooker, layering as flat as possible.

2. Combine soy sauce, brown sugar, oil and garlic in small bowl. Reserve ⅓ cup sauce; set aside. Pour remaining sauce over skewers. Cover; cook on LOW 2 hours. Turn skewers over; cook 1 hour longer.

3. Transfer skewers to serving platter. Discard cooking liquid. Pour reserved sauce over skewers; sprinkle with green onions, if desired, and sesame seeds.

Makes 4 to 6 servings

Prep Time: 10 minutes
Cook Time: 3 hours (LOW)

Sun-Dried Tomato Appetizer Torte

3 cups chopped onion
3 jars (about 7 ounces each) oil-packed sun-dried tomatoes,
  drained and finely chopped
3 tablespoons sugar
1 tablespoon minced garlic
1 piece (2 inches) fresh ginger, peeled and grated
1 teaspoon herbes de Provence
½ teaspoon salt
½ cup red wine vinegar
1 package (8 ounces) cream cheese
  Fresh basil sprigs (optional)
  Assorted crackers

1. Place onion, tomatoes, sugar, garlic, ginger, herbes de Provence and salt in slow cooker. Pour in red wine vinegar; stir gently to mix. Cover; cook on LOW 4 to 5 hours or on HIGH 3 hours, stirring occasionally. Let mixture cool before using.

2. To serve, slice cream cheese in half horizontally (use dental floss for clean cut). Spread ⅓ cup tomato mixture onto one cream cheese half. Top with second cream cheese half and spread ⅓ cup tomato mixture on top. Garnish with fresh basil sprigs and serve with crackers. Refrigerate or freeze remaining tomato mixture for another use.   *Makes 8 servings*

Prep Time: 10 minutes
Cook Time: 4 to 5 hours (LOW) or 3 hours (HIGH)

Tip: Use leftover tomato mixture as a topping for bruschetta or toss with hot cooked pasta.

Steamed Pork Buns

½ container (18 ounces) refrigerated shredded cooked pork in barbecue sauce*
1 tablespoon Asian garlic chili sauce
1 package (about 16 ounces) refrigerated biscuit dough (8 large biscuits)
  Dipping Sauce (recipe follows)
  Sliced green onions (optional)

*Look for pork in plain, not smoky, barbecue sauce. Substitute chicken in barbecue sauce, if desired.

1. Combine pork and chili sauce in medium bowl. Split biscuits in half. Roll or stretch each biscuit into 4-inch circle. Spoon 1 tablespoon pork onto center of each biscuit. Gather edges around filling and press to seal.

2. Generously butter 2-quart baking dish that fits inside 5- or 6-quart slow cooker. Arrange filled biscuits in single layer, overlapping slightly if necessary. Cover dish with buttered foil, buttered side down.

3. Place small rack in slow cooker. Add 1 inch hot water (water should not come to top of rack). Place baking dish on rack. Cover; cook on HIGH 2 hours.

4. Meanwhile, prepare Dipping Sauce. Garnish pork buns with green onions. Serve with Dipping Sauce. *Makes 8 servings*

Dipping Sauce: Stir together 2 tablespoons rice vinegar, 2 tablespoons soy sauce, 4 teaspoons sugar and 1 teaspoon toasted sesame oil in small bowl until sugar dissolves. Sprinkle with 1 tablespoon minced green onion (green part only) just before serving.

Caponata

1 medium eggplant (about 1 pound), peeled and cut into ½-inch pieces
1 can (about 14 ounces) diced Italian plum tomatoes
1 medium onion, chopped
1 red bell pepper, cut into ½-inch pieces
½ cup salsa
¼ cup olive oil
2 tablespoons capers, drained
2 tablespoons balsamic vinegar
3 cloves garlic, minced
1 teaspoon dried oregano
¼ teaspoon salt
⅓ cup packed fresh basil, cut into thin strips
   Toasted Italian or French bread slices

1. Combine eggplant, tomatoes, onion, bell pepper, salsa, oil, capers, vinegar, garlic, oregano and salt in slow cooker. Cover; cook on LOW 7 to 8 hours or until vegetables are crisp-tender.

2. Stir in basil. Serve at room temperature on toasted bread.   *Makes about 5¼ cups*

Tip: Be sure to cut all of the ingredients for the Caponata into uniform pieces. This allows them to cook evenly in the slow cooker.

Swiss Cheese Fondue

1 clove garlic, cut in half
1 can (10½ ounces) CAMPBELL'S® Condensed Chicken Broth
2 cans (10¾ ounces each) CAMPBELL'S® Condensed Cheddar Cheese Soup
1 cup water
½ cup Chablis or other dry white wine
1 tablespoon Dijon-style mustard
1 tablespoon cornstarch
1 pound shredded Emmentaler or Gruyère cheese, at room temperature
¼ teaspoon ground nutmeg
   Dash ground black pepper
   PEPPERIDGE FARM® Garlic Bread, baked and cut into cubes
   Fresh vegetables for dipping

1. Rub the inside of a 5½- to 6-quart slow cooker with the cut sides of the garlic. Discard the garlic. Stir the broth, soup, water, wine, mustard, cornstarch, cheese, nutmeg and black pepper in the cooker.

2. Cover and cook on LOW for 1 hour or until the cheese is melted, stirring occasionally.

3. Serve with the bread and vegetables on skewers for dipping.   *Makes 6 servings*

Prep Time: 10 minutes
Cook Time: 1 hour

CAMPBELL'S® Kitchen Tip: This recipe may be doubled.

Honey-Mustard Chicken Wings

3 pounds chicken wings
1 teaspoon salt
1 teaspoon black pepper
½ cup honey
½ cup barbecue sauce
2 tablespoons spicy brown mustard
1 clove garlic, minced
3 to 4 thin lemon slices

1. Cut off chicken wing tips; discard. Cut each wing at joint to make two pieces. Sprinkle with salt and pepper; place wing pieces on broiler rack. Broil 4 to 5 inches from heat about 10 minutes, turning halfway through cooking time. Place in slow cooker.

2. Combine honey, barbecue sauce, mustard and garlic in small bowl; mix well. Pour sauce over chicken wings. Top with lemon slices. Cover; cook on LOW 4 to 5 hours.

3. Remove and discard lemon slices. Serve wings with sauce from slow cooker.

Makes about 24 wings

Prep Time: 20 minutes
Cook Time: 4 to 5 hours (LOW)

Tip: Browning the chicken wings in the broiler before cooking them in the slow cooker is not necessary, but will enhance their flavor and appearance.

Easy Party Meatballs

1 jar (1 pound 10 ounces) PREGO® Marinara Italian Sauce
1 jar (12 ounces) grape jelly
½ cup prepared chili sauce
2½ pounds frozen fully-cooked meatballs, cocktail size

1. Stir the Italian sauce, jelly, chili sauce and meatballs in a 4½-quart slow cooker.

2. Cover and cook on LOW for 6 to 7 hours* or until the meatballs are cooked through. Serve the meatballs on a serving plate with toothpicks.   *Makes 8 servings*

*Or on HIGH for 3 to 4 hours.

Prep Time: 5 minutes
Cook Time: 6 to 7 hours

CAMPBELL'S® Kitchen Tips: Larger-size or turkey meatballs can also be used, if desired. For a special touch, serve with cranberry chutney for dipping.

Spicy, Sweet & Sour Cocktail Franks

2 packages (8 ounces each) cocktail franks
½ cup ketchup or chili sauce
½ cup apricot preserves
1 teaspoon hot pepper sauce
   Additional hot pepper sauce (optional)

1. Combine all ingredients in 1½-quart slow cooker; mix well. Cover; cook on LOW 2 to 3 hours.

2. Serve warm or at room temperature with additional hot pepper sauce, if desired.
                        Makes about 4 dozen cocktail franks

Prep Time: 8 minutes
Cook Time: 2 to 3 hours (LOW)

Tomato Topping for Bruschetta

3 medium tomatoes, peeled, cored, seeded and diced
1 stalk celery, chopped
1 shallot, chopped
2 pepperoncini peppers, chopped*
1 teaspoon tomato paste
½ teaspoon salt
¼ teaspoon black pepper
1 tablespoon olive oil
4 large slices Italian or French bread
1 clove garlic

Pepperoncini are pickled peppers sold in jars with brine. They are available in the condiment aisle of the supermarket.

1. Drain any tomato juices. Combine tomatoes, celery, shallot, pepperoncini peppers, tomato paste, salt, black pepper and oil in slow cooker. Cover; cook on LOW 45 minutes to 1 hour.

2. Toast bread. Immediately rub with garlic. Spread tomato topping on bread. Serve immediately.   *Makes 4 servings*

Prep Time: 10 minutes
Cook Time: 45 minutes to 1 hour (LOW)

Brats in Beer

1½ pounds bratwurst (about 5 or 6 links)
1 bottle (12 ounces) amber ale
1 medium onion, thinly sliced
2 tablespoons packed brown sugar
2 tablespoons red wine vinegar or cider vinegar
Spicy brown mustard
Cocktail rye bread

1. Combine bratwurst, ale, onion, brown sugar and vinegar in slow cooker. Cover; cook on LOW 4 to 5 hours.

2. Remove bratwurst and onion slices from slow cooker. Cut bratwurst into ½-inch-thick slices. For mini open-faced sandwiches, spread mustard on cocktail rye bread. Top with bratwurst slices and onion.   *Makes 30 to 36 appetizers*

Prep Time: 5 minutes
Cook Time: 4 to 5 hours

Tip: Choose a light-tasting beer for cooking brats. Hearty ales can leave the meat tasting slightly bitter.

Soups &
SANDWICHES

Simmering Hot & Sour Soup

  2 cans (about 14 ounces each) chicken broth
  1 cup chopped cooked chicken or pork
  4 ounces fresh shiitake mushroom caps, thinly sliced
  ½ cup sliced bamboo shoots, cut into thin strips
  3 tablespoons rice wine vinegar
  2 tablespoons soy sauce
1½ teaspoons Chinese chili paste *or* 1 teaspoon hot chili oil
  4 ounces firm tofu, well drained and cut into ½-inch pieces
  2 teaspoons dark sesame oil
  2 tablespoons cornstarch
  2 tablespoons cold water
     Chopped cilantro or sliced green onions (optional)

1. Combine broth, chicken, mushrooms, bamboo shoots, vinegar, soy sauce and chili paste in slow cooker. Cover; cook on LOW 3 to 4 hours.

2. Stir in tofu and sesame oil. Blend cornstarch and water in small bowl until smooth. Stir into slow cooker. Cover; cook on HIGH 15 minutes or until soup is thickened.

3. Serve hot; garnish with cilantro.   *Makes 4 servings*

Burgundy Beef Po' Boys with Dipping Sauce

1 boneless beef chuck shoulder or bottom round roast (3 pounds)
2 cups chopped onions
¼ cup red wine
3 tablespoons balsamic vinegar
1 tablespoon beef bouillon granules
1 tablespoon Worcestershire sauce
¾ teaspoon dried thyme
½ teaspoon garlic powder
Italian rolls, warmed and split

1. Cut beef into 3 or 4 pieces; trim fat. Place onions in slow cooker. Top with beef, wine, vinegar, bouillon, Worcestershire, thyme and garlic powder. Cover; cook on HIGH 8 to 10 hours or until beef is very tender.

2. Remove beef; cool slightly and remove excess fat. Shred with two forks.

3. Let cooking liquid stand 5 minutes. Skim off fat. Serve beef on rolls. Serve with cooking liquid as dipping sauce. *Makes 6 to 8 sandwiches*

BURGUNDY BEEF PO' BOY WITH DIPPING SAUCE

Mediterranean Shrimp Soup

2 cans (about 14 ounces each) chicken broth
1 can (about 14 ounces) diced tomatoes
1 can (8 ounces) tomato sauce
1 medium onion, chopped
½ medium green bell pepper, chopped
½ cup orange juice
½ cup dry white wine (optional)
1 jar (2½ ounces) sliced mushrooms
¼ cup sliced pitted black olives
2 cloves garlic, minced
1 teaspoon dried basil
2 bay leaves
¼ teaspoon whole fennel seeds, crushed
⅛ teaspoon black pepper
1 pound medium raw shrimp, peeled and deveined

1. Place all ingredients except shrimp in slow cooker. Cover; cook on LOW 4 to 4½ hours or until vegetables are crisp-tender.

2. Stir in shrimp. Cover; cook 15 to 30 minutes or until shrimp are pink and opaque. Remove and discard bay leaves. *Makes 6 servings*

Tip: For a heartier soup, add 1 pound of firm white fish, such as cod or haddock, cut into 1-inch pieces. Add the fish to the slow cooker 45 minutes before serving. Cook, covered, on LOW.

Hot Beef Sandwiches

1 beef chuck roast (3 to 4 pounds), cut into chunks
1 jar (6 ounces) sliced dill pickles, undrained
1 can (about 14 ounces) crushed tomatoes with Italian seasoning
1 medium onion, diced
4 cloves garlic, minced
1 teaspoon mustard seeds
   Hamburger buns

1. Place beef in slow cooker. Pour pickles with juice over beef. Add tomatoes, onion, garlic and mustard seeds.

2. Cover; cook on LOW 8 to 10 hours.

3. Remove beef from slow cooker. Shred beef with two forks. Return beef to tomato mixture; mix well. Serve beef mixture on buns. *Makes 6 to 8 servings*

Serving Suggestion: Garnish with lettuce, sliced tomatoes, red onion slices, shredded slaw or other fixings to taste.

HOT BEEF SANDWICH

Fennel Soup au Gratin

8 cups SWANSON® Beef Broth (Regular, 50% Less Sodium or Certified Organic)
2 tablespoons dry sherry
2 teaspoons dried thyme leaves, crushed
3 tablespoons butter
1 bulb fennel, sliced (about 4 cups)
2 medium onions, sliced (about 4 cups)
8 ounces French bread, sliced ½-inch thick
½ cup shredded Italian blend cheese

1. Stir the broth, sherry, thyme, butter, fennel and onions in a 5½-quart slow cooker. Cover and cook on HIGH for 6 hours.

2. Just before serving, top **each** bread slice with **1 tablespoon** of the cheese. Place the bread on a baking sheet. Broil 4 inches from the heat for 1 minute or until golden.

3. Divide the soup mixture among **8** serving bowls. Top **each** serving of soup with a cheese toast.   *Makes 8 servings*

Prep Time: 15 minutes
Cook Time: 6 hours

FENNEL SOUP AU GRATIN

Tavern Burger

2 pounds 95% lean ground beef
½ cup ketchup
¼ cup packed brown sugar
¼ cup yellow mustard
    Hamburger buns

1. Brown beef 6 to 8 minutes in medium skillet over medium-high heat, stirring to break up meat. Drain fat. Transfer beef to slow cooker.

2. Add ketchup, brown sugar and mustard; mix well. Cover; cook on LOW 4 to 6 hours. Serve on buns.   *Makes 8 servings*

Variation: For added flavor, add a can of pork and beans with the beef.

Fiesta Black Bean Soup

6 cups chicken broth
12 ounces potatoes, peeled and diced
1 can (about 15 ounces) black beans, rinsed and drained
½ pound cooked ham, diced
½ onion, diced
1 can (4 ounces) chopped jalapeño peppers
2 cloves garlic, minced
2 teaspoons dried oregano
1½ teaspoons dried thyme
1 teaspoon ground cumin
    Toppings: sour cream, chopped bell pepper and chopped tomatoes (optional)

1. Combine broth, potatoes, beans, ham, onion, jalapeños, garlic, oregano, thyme and cumin in slow cooker; mix well.

2. Cover; cook on LOW 8 to 10 hours or on HIGH 4 to 5 hours.

3. Adjust seasonings. Serve with desired toppings.   *Makes 6 to 8 servings*

Italian Beef and Barley Soup

1 boneless beef top sirloin steak (about 1½ pounds)
1 tablespoon vegetable oil
4 medium carrots or parsnips, cut into ¼-inch slices
1 cup chopped onion
1 teaspoon dried thyme
½ teaspoon dried rosemary
¼ teaspoon black pepper
⅓ cup uncooked pearl barley
2 cans (about 14 ounces each) beef broth
1 can (about 14 ounces) diced tomatoes with Italian seasoning

1. Cut beef into 1-inch pieces. Heat oil over medium-high heat in large skillet. Brown beef on all sides; set aside.

2. Place carrots and onion in slow cooker; sprinkle with thyme, rosemary and pepper. Top with barley and beef. Pour broth and tomatoes over beef.

3. Cover; cook on LOW 8 to 10 hours or until beef is tender.   *Makes 6 servings*

Prep Time: 20 minutes
Cook Time: 8 to 10 hours (LOW)

Tip: Choose pearl barley rather than quick-cooking barley, because it will stand up to longer cooking.

Hot & Juicy Reuben Sandwiches

1 mild-cure corned beef (about 1½ pounds)
2 cups sauerkraut, drained
½ cup beef broth
1 small onion, sliced
1 clove garlic, minced
¼ teaspoon caraway seeds
4 to 6 peppercorns
8 slices pumpernickel or rye bread
4 slices Swiss cheese
Mustard

1. Trim excess fat from corned beef. Place beef in slow cooker. Add sauerkraut, broth, onion, garlic, caraway seeds and peppercorns.

2. Cover; cook on LOW 7 to 9 hours.

3. Remove beef from slow cooker. Cut across the grain into ¼-inch-thick slices. Divide evenly among 4 slices of bread. Top each slice with ½ cup drained sauerkraut mixture and 1 slice of cheese. Spread mustard on remaining 4 bread slices. Close sandwiches. *Makes 4 servings*

Prep Time: 25 minutes
Cook Time: 7 to 9 hours (LOW)

Slow-Cooked Pulled Pork Sandwiches

1 tablespoon vegetable oil
1 (3½- to 4-pound) boneless pork shoulder roast, netted or tied
1 can (10½ ounces) CAMPBELL'S® Condensed French Onion Soup
1 cup ketchup
¼ cup cider vinegar
3 tablespoons packed brown sugar
12 round sandwich rolls, split

1. Heat the oil in a 10-inch skillet over medium-high heat. Add the roast and cook until it's well browned on all sides.

2. Stir the soup, ketchup, vinegar and brown sugar in a 5-quart slow cooker. Add the roast and turn to coat with the soup mixture.

3. Cover and cook on LOW for 8 to 10 hours* or until the meat is fork-tender.

4. Remove the roast from the cooker to a cutting board and let it stand for 10 minutes. Using 2 forks, shred the pork. Return the shredded pork to the cooker.

5. Divide the pork and sauce mixture among the rolls.   *Makes 12 sandwiches*

Or on HIGH for 4 to 5 hours.

Start to Finish Time: 8 to 10 hours, 25 minutes
Prepping: 15 minutes
Cooking: 8 to 10 hours
Standing: 10 minutes

SLOW-COOKED PULLED PORK SANDWICH

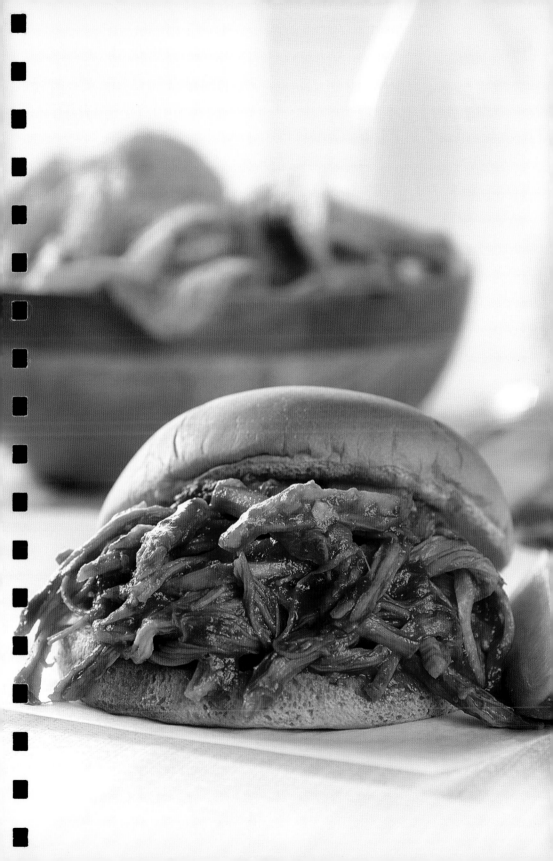

Dinner CREATIONS

Lemon Pork Chops

1 tablespoon vegetable oil
4 boneless pork chops
3 cans (8 ounces each) tomato sauce
1 large onion, quartered and sliced (optional)
1 large green bell pepper, cut into strips
1 tablespoon lemon-pepper seasoning
1 tablespoon Worcestershire sauce
1 lemon, quartered
   Lemon wedges (optional)

1. Heat oil in large skillet over medium heat. Brown pork chops on both sides. Drain fat. Transfer pork chops to slow cooker.

2. Combine tomato sauce, onion, if desired, bell pepper, lemon-pepper seasoning and Worcestershire sauce in medium bowl. Add to slow cooker.

3. Squeeze juice from lemon quarters over mixture; place squeezed lemon quarters in slow cooker. Cover; cook on LOW 6 to 8 hours or until pork is tender. Remove lemon wedges before serving. Garnish with additional lemon wedges.   *Makes 4 servings*

Prep Time: 10 minutes
Cook Time: 6 to 8 hours (LOW)

Serving Suggestions: Great served with green beans and couscous.

Forty-Clove Chicken

1 whole chicken (3 pounds), cut up
  Salt and black pepper
1 to 2 tablespoons olive oil
¼ cup dry white wine
2 tablespoons chopped fresh parsley *or* 2 teaspoons dried parsley
2 tablespoons dry vermouth
2 teaspoons dried basil
1 teaspoon dried oregano
  Pinch red pepper flakes
40 cloves garlic (about 2 bulbs), peeled
4 stalks celery, sliced
  Juice and peel of 1 lemon

1. Remove skin from chicken. Sprinkle chicken with salt and pepper. Heat oil in large skillet over medium heat. Add chicken; brown on all sides. Remove to platter.

2. Combine wine, parsley, vermouth, basil, oregano and red pepper flakes in large bowl. Add garlic and celery; coat well. Transfer garlic and celery to slow cooker with slotted spoon. Add chicken to remaining herb mixture; coat well. Place chicken on top of celery mixture in slow cooker. Sprinkle lemon juice and peel over chicken. Cover; cook on LOW 6 hours.   *Makes 4 to 6 servings*

Curry Beef

1 pound 90% lean ground beef
1 medium onion, thinly sliced
½ cup beef broth
1 tablespoon curry powder
1 teaspoon ground cumin
2 cloves garlic, minced
1 cup sour cream
¼ cup milk
½ cup raisins, divided
1 teaspoon sugar
12 ounces uncooked wide egg noodles *or* 1⅓ cups uncooked
    long grain white rice
¼ cup chopped walnuts, almonds or pecans

1. Brown beef 6 to 8 minutes in large skillet over medium-high heat, stirring to break up meat. Drain fat. Combine beef, onion, broth, curry powder, cumin and garlic in slow cooker. Cover; cook on LOW 4 hours.

2. Stir in sour cream, milk, ¼ cup raisins and sugar. Cover; cook 30 minutes or until thickened and heated through.

3. Cook noodles according to package directions; drain. Spoon beef curry over noodles. Sprinkle with remaining ¼ cup raisins and walnuts. *Makes 4 servings*

Serving Suggestion: Serve with sliced cucumber sprinkled with sugar and vinegar or plain yogurt topped with brown sugar, chopped bananas and green onions.

Italian Meatballs & Peppers

**2 cans (28 ounces each) HUNT'S® Diced Tomatoes with Basil, Garlic &
    Oregano, undrained**
1 can (6 ounces) HUNT'S® Tomato Paste
1 package (16 ounces) frozen cooked meatballs
1 package (14 ounces) frozen bell pepper strips

1. Combine tomatoes, tomato paste, meatballs and pepper strips in slow cooker.

2. Cook on LOW setting for 8 to 10 hours or on HIGH setting for 4 to 6 hours.
Makes 8 servings (1 cup each with 4 meatballs)

Prep Time: 10 minutes
Total Time: 8 hours

Harvest Ham Supper

6 carrots, cut into 2-inch pieces
3 medium sweet potatoes, quartered
1 to 1½ pounds boneless ham
1 cup maple syrup

1. Place carrots and potatoes in bottom of slow cooker. Place ham on top of vegetables.
Pour syrup over ham and vegetables.

2. Cover; cook on LOW 6 to 8 hours.   *Makes 6 servings*

Prep Time: 10 minutes
Cook Time: 6 to 8 hours (LOW)

Fiery Chili Beef

1 to 2 beef flank steaks (1 to 1½ pounds)
1 can (28 ounces) diced tomatoes
1 can (15 ounces) pinto beans, rinsed and drained
1 medium onion, chopped
2 cloves garlic, minced
½ teaspoon salt
½ teaspoon ground cumin
¼ teaspoon black pepper
1 canned chipotle chile pepper in adobo sauce
1 teaspoon adobo sauce from canned chile pepper
Flour tortillas (optional)

1. Cut flank steak into 6 equal pieces. Combine flank steak, tomatoes, beans, onion, garlic, salt, cumin and black pepper in slow cooker.

2. Dice chile pepper. Add pepper and adobo sauce to slow cooker; mix well.

3. Cover; cook on LOW 7 to 8 hours. Serve with tortillas, if desired.

Makes 6 servings

Prep Time: 15 minutes
Cook Time: 7 to 8 hours (LOW)

Tip: Chipotle chile peppers are dried, smoked jalapeño peppers with a very hot yet smoky, sweet flavor. They can be found dried, pickled and canned in adobo sauce.

Southwestern Stuffed Peppers

4 green bell peppers
1 can (about 15 ounces) black beans, rinsed and drained
1 cup (4 ounces) shredded pepper jack cheese
¾ cup salsa
½ cup frozen corn
½ cup chopped green onions
⅓ cup uncooked long grain converted white rice
1 teaspoon chili powder
½ teaspoon ground cumin
Sour cream (optional)

1. Cut thin slice off top of each bell pepper. Carefully remove seeds, leaving peppers whole.

2. Combine beans, cheese, salsa, corn, green onions, rice, chili powder and cumin in medium bowl. Spoon filling evenly into peppers. Place peppers in slow cooker. Cover; cook on LOW 4 to 6 hours. Serve with sour cream, if desired.   *Makes 4 servings*

Prep Time: 15 minutes
Cook Time: 4 to 6 hours (LOW)

Chicken Cacciatore

1½ cups SWANSON® Chicken Stock
2 teaspoons garlic powder
2 cans (14½ ounces each) diced Italian-style tomatoes
4 cups mushrooms, cut in half (about 12 ounces)
2 large onions, chopped (about 2 cups)
3 pounds chicken parts, skin removed
¼ cup cornstarch
10 cups hot cooked spaghetti

1. Stir **1 cup** stock, garlic powder, tomatoes, mushrooms and onions in a 5- to 6-quart slow cooker. Add the chicken and turn to coat.

2. Cover and cook on LOW for 7 to 8 hours* or until the chicken is cooked through. Remove the chicken from the cooker and keep warm.

3. Stir the cornstarch and remaining stock in a small bowl until the mixture is smooth. Stir the cornstarch mixture in the cooker. Cover and cook on HIGH for 10 minutes or until the mixture boils and thickens. Serve with the chicken and spaghetti.

Makes 6 servings

Or on HIGH for 4 to 5 hours.

Prep Time: 10 minutes
Cook Time: 8 hours

Serving Suggestions: Serve with a tomato and cucumber salad with fresh basil and Italian viniagrette. For dessert serve almond biscotti.

Sweet 'n' Spicy Ribs

5 cups barbecue sauce
¾ cup packed brown sugar
¼ cup honey
2 tablespoons Cajun seasoning
1 tablespoon garlic powder
1 tablespoon onion powder
6 pounds pork or beef back ribs, cut into 3-rib or individual rib portions

1. Stir together barbecue sauce, brown sugar, honey, Cajun seasoning, garlic powder and onion powder in medium bowl. Reserve 1 cup mixture for dipping sauce; refrigerate until ready to serve.

2. Place ribs in slow cooker. Pour remaining barbecue sauce mixture over ribs. Cover; cook on LOW 8 hours or until meat is very tender.

3. Serve ribs with reserved sauce.   *Makes 10 servings*

Prep Time: 10 to 15 minutes
Cook Time: 8 hours (LOW)

Tip: To make the slow cooker cleanup easier, spray the inside with nonstick cooking spray before adding any of the ingredients.

Beef and Vegetables in Rich Burgundy Sauce

1 package (8 ounces) baby carrots
1 package (8 ounces) sliced mushrooms
1 medium green bell pepper, cut into thin strips
1 boneless beef chuck roast (2½ pounds)
1 can (10¾ ounces) condensed golden mushroom soup, undiluted
¼ cup dry red wine or beef broth
1 package (1 ounce) dry onion soup mix
1 tablespoon Worcestershire sauce
¼ teaspoon black pepper
3 tablespoons cornstarch
2 tablespoons water
4 cups hot cooked noodles
   Chopped fresh parsley (optional)

1. Place carrots, mushrooms and bell pepper in slow cooker. Place roast on top of vegetables. Combine mushroom soup, wine, soup mix, Worcestershire sauce and black pepper in medium bowl; mix well. Pour soup mixture over roast. Cover; cook on LOW 8 to 10 hours.

2. Transfer roast to cutting board; cover with foil. Let stand 10 to 15 minutes before slicing.

3. Blend cornstarch and water until smooth; stir into slow cooker. Cook, uncovered, 15 minutes or until thickened. Serve beef and vegetables with sauce over cooked noodles. Garnish with parsley.   *Makes 6 to 8 servings*

On the SIDE

Barley with Currants and Pine Nuts

1 tablespoon butter
1 small onion, finely chopped
2 cups chicken or vegetable broth
½ cup pearled barley
½ teaspoon salt
¼ teaspoon black pepper
⅓ cup currants
¼ cup pine nuts

1. Melt butter in small skillet over medium-high heat. Add onion. Cook and stir 2 minutes or until lightly browned. Transfer to slow cooker. Add broth, barley, salt and pepper. Stir in currants. Cover; cook on LOW 3 hours.

2. Stir in pine nuts; serve immediately.   *Makes 4 servings*

Prep Time: 10 minutes
Cook Time: 3 hours (LOW)

Rustic Cheddar Mashed Potatoes

2 pounds russet potatoes, peeled and diced
1 cup water
⅓ cup butter, cut into small pieces
½ to ¾ cup milk
1¼ teaspoons salt
½ teaspoon black pepper
½ cup finely chopped green onions
¾ cup (3 ounces) shredded Cheddar cheese

1. Combine potatoes and water in slow cooker; dot with butter. Cover; cook on LOW 6 hours or on HIGH 3 hours or until potatoes are tender. Remove potatoes to large mixing bowl.

2. Beat potatoes with electric mixer at medium speed until fluffy. Add milk, salt and pepper; beat until smooth.

3. Stir in green onions and cheese; cover. Let stand 15 minutes to allow flavors to blend and cheese to melt.   *Makes 8 servings*

Tip: To easily and thoroughly dot the potatoes with butter, grate cold butter with the large holes of a box grater directly over the potatoes.

Five-Bean Casserole

2 medium onions, chopped

8 ounces bacon, diced

2 cloves garlic, minced

½ cup packed brown sugar

½ cup cider vinegar

1 teaspoon salt

1 teaspoon dry mustard

¼ teaspoon black pepper

2 cans (about 15 ounces each) kidney beans, rinsed and drained

1 can (about 15 ounces) chickpeas, rinsed and drained

1 can (about 15 ounces) butter beans, rinsed and drained

1 can (about 15 ounces) Great Northern or cannellini beans, rinsed and drained

1 can (about 15 ounces) baked beans

1. Cook and stir onions, bacon and garlic in large skillet over medium heat until onions are tender; drain. Stir in brown sugar, vinegar, salt, mustard and pepper. Simmer over low heat 15 minutes.

2. Combine beans in slow cooker. Spoon onion mixture evenly over top. Cover; cook on LOW 6 to 8 hours or on HIGH 3 to 4 hours.   *Makes 16 servings*

Spinach Spoon Bread

1 package (10 ounces) frozen chopped spinach, thawed and squeezed dry
1 red bell pepper, diced
4 eggs, lightly beaten
1 cup cottage cheese
1 package (5½ ounces) cornbread mix
6 green onions, sliced
½ cup (1 stick) butter, melted
1¼ teaspoons seasoned salt

1. Lightly grease slow cooker. Turn heat to HIGH.

2. Combine all ingredients in large bowl; mix well. Pour batter into prepared slow cooker. Place lid on slow cooker slightly ajar to allow excess moisture to escape. Cook on LOW 3 to 4 hours or on HIGH 1¾ to 2 hours or until edges are golden and knife inserted into center of bread comes out clean.

3. To serve, scoop bread from slow cooker with spoon. Or, loosen edges and bottom with knife and invert onto plate; cut into wedges.   *Makes 8 servings*

Tip: Spoon bread is a soft, moist egg-based dish made with cornmeal and sometimes corn kernels. It is more like a pudding than a bread and, as its name indicates, can be served with a spoon.

Scalloped Potatoes

Vegetable cooking spray
3 pounds Yukon Gold or Eastern potatoes, thinly sliced (about 9 cups)
1 large onion, thinly sliced (about 1 cup)
1 can (10¾ ounces) CAMPBELL'S® Condensed Cream of Mushroom Soup
    (Regular, 98% Fat Free or 25% Less Sodium)
½ cup CAMPBELL'S® Condensed Chicken Broth
1 cup shredded Cheddar or crumbled blue cheese (about 4 ounces)

1. Spray the inside of a 6-quart slow cooker with the cooking spray. Layer a third of the potatoes and half of the onion in the cooker. Repeat the layers. Top with the remaining potatoes.

2. Stir the soup and broth in a small bowl. Pour over the potatoes. Cover and cook on HIGH for 4 to 5 hours or until the potatoes are tender.

3. Top the potatoes with the cheese. Cover and let stand for 5 minutes or until the cheese is melted.   *Makes 6 servings*

Prep Time: 15 minutes
Cook Time: 4 to 5 hours
Stand Time: 5 minutes

Cheesy Corn and Peppers

2 pounds frozen corn kernels
2 poblano peppers, chopped *or* 1 large green bell pepper and 1 jalapeño pepper,*
   seeded and finely chopped
2 tablespoons butter, cubed
1 teaspoon salt
½ teaspoon ground cumin
¼ teaspoon black pepper
1 cup (4 ounces) shredded sharp Cheddar cheese
3 ounces cream cheese, cubed

*Jalapeño peppers can sting and irritate the skin, so wear rubber gloves when handling peppers and do not touch your eyes. Wash hands after handling.

1. Coat slow cooker with nonstick cooking spray. Add corn, poblanos, butter, salt, cumin and black pepper. Cover; cook on HIGH 2 hours.

2. Add cheeses; stir to blend. Cover; cook 15 minutes more or until cheeses melt.

Makes 8 servings

Prep Time: 8 minutes
Cook Time: 2¼ hours (HIGH)

Winter Squash and Apples

1 teaspoon salt
½ teaspoon black pepper
1 butternut squash (about 2 pounds), peeled and seeded
2 apples, cored and cut into slices
1 medium onion, quartered and sliced
2 tablespoons butter

1. Combine salt and pepper in small bowl; set aside.

2. Cut squash into 2-inch pieces; place in slow cooker. Add apples and onion. Sprinkle with salt mixture; stir well. Cover; cook on LOW 6 to 7 hours or until vegetables are tender.

3. Stir in butter just before serving; season to taste with additional salt and pepper.

Makes 4 to 6 servings

Prep Time: 15 minutes
Cook Time: 6 to 7 hours (LOW)

Variation: Add ¼ to ½ cup packed brown sugar and ½ teaspoon ground cinnamon with butter in step 3; mix well. Cook an additional 15 minutes.

Risotto-Style Peppered Rice

1 cup uncooked long grain rice
1 green bell pepper, chopped
1 red bell pepper, chopped
1 cup chopped onion
½ teaspoon ground turmeric
⅛ teaspoon ground red pepper (optional)
1 can (about 14 ounces) chicken or vegetable broth
4 ounces pepper jack cheese, cubed
½ cup milk
¼ cup (½ stick) butter, cubed
1 teaspoon salt

1. Place rice, bell peppers, onions, turmeric and ground red pepper, if desired, in slow cooker. Stir in broth. Cover; cook on LOW 4 to 5 hours.

2. Stir in cheese, milk, butter and salt; fluff rice with fork. Cover; cook on LOW 5 minutes or until cheese melts.   *Makes 4 to 6 servings*

Lemon-Mint Red Potatoes

2 pounds new red potatoes
3 tablespoons extra-virgin olive oil
¾ teaspoon dried Greek seasoning or dried oregano
¼ teaspoon garlic powder
1 teaspoon salt
¼ teaspoon black pepper
1 teaspoon grated lemon peel
2 tablespoons lemon juice
2 tablespoons butter
4 tablespoons chopped fresh mint, divided

1. Coat inside of 6-quart slow cooker with nonstick cooking spray. Add potatoes and oil, stirring gently to coat. Sprinkle with Greek seasoning, garlic powder, salt and pepper. Cover; cook on LOW 7 hours or on HIGH 4 hours.

2. Stir in lemon peel, lemon juice, butter and 2 tablespoons mint until butter is completely melted. Cover; cook 15 minutes to allow flavors to blend. Sprinkle with remaining mint.   *Makes 4 servings*

Prep Time: 25 minutes
Cook Time: 7¼ hours (LOW) or 4¼ hours (HIGH)

*Tip: It's easy to prepare this recipe ahead of time; simply
follow instructions as listed and then turn off heat and
let stand at room temperature for up to 2 hours.
Reheat or serve at room temperature.*

Polenta-Style Corn Casserole

1 can (about 14 ounces) vegetable or chicken broth
½ cup cornmeal
1 can (7 ounces) corn, drained
1 can (4 ounces) diced green chiles, drained
¼ cup diced red bell pepper
½ teaspoon salt
¼ teaspoon black pepper
1 cup (4 ounces) shredded Cheddar cheese

1. Pour broth into slow cooker. Whisk in cornmeal. Add corn, chiles, bell pepper, salt and pepper. Cover; cook on LOW 4 to 5 hours or on HIGH 2 to 3 hours.

2. Stir in cheese. Cook, uncovered, 15 to 30 minutes or until cheese melts.

Makes 6 servings

Serving Suggestion: Divide cooked corn mixture into lightly greased individual ramekins or spread in pie plate; cover and refrigerate. Serve at room temperature or warm in oven or microwave.

POLENTA-STYLE CORN CASSEROLE

Sweet
ENDINGS

Easy Chocolate Pudding Cake

1 package (6-serving size) instant chocolate pudding and pie filling mix
3 cups milk
1 package (about 18 ounces) chocolate fudge cake mix plus ingredients to
    prepare mix
  Whipped topping or ice cream (optional)
  Crushed peppermint candies (optional)

1. Spray 4-quart slow cooker with nonstick cooking spray. Place pudding mix in slow cooker. Whisk in milk.

2. Prepare cake mix according to package directions. Carefully pour cake mix into slow cooker. Do not stir. Cover; cook on HIGH 1½ hours or until cake is set. Serve warm with whipped topping and candies, if desired.   *Makes about 16 servings*

Prep Time: 15 minutes
Cook Time: 1½ hours (HIGH)

Cherry Rice Pudding

1½ cups milk
1 cup hot cooked rice
3 eggs, beaten
½ cup sugar
¼ cup dried cherries
½ teaspoon almond extract
¼ teaspoon salt

1. Combine all ingredients in large bowl. Pour mixture into greased 1½-quart casserole. Cover with foil.

2. Place rack in 5-quart slow cooker and pour in 1 cup water. Place casserole on rack. Cover; cook on LOW 4 to 5 hours.

3. Remove casserole from slow cooker. Let stand 15 minutes before serving.

Makes 6 servings

Variation: Try substituting dried cranberries for the dried cherries or add 2 tablespoons each for a delicious new dish.

Raisin Cinnamon Bread Pudding

Vegetable cooking spray
10 slices PEPPERIDGE FARM® Raisin Cinnamon Swirl Bread, cut into cubes
     (about 5 cups)
 1 can (14 ounces) sweetened condensed milk
 1 cup water
 1 teaspoon vanilla extract
 4 eggs, beaten
   Ice cream (optional)

1. Spray the inside of a 4½- to 5-quart slow cooker with cooking spray.

2. Place the bread in slow cooker.

3. Stir the milk, water, vanilla and eggs with a whisk or fork in a medium bowl. Pour over the bread mixture. Stir and push the bread cubes into milk mixture to coat.

4. Cover and cook on LOW for 2½ to 3 hours or until set. Serve warm with ice cream, if desired.   *Makes 6 servings*

Prep Time: 10 minutes
Cook Time: 2½ to 3 hours

*Tip: Even when it's too hot to bake, you can surprise
your family with fresh, homemade desserts
made in the slow cooker.*

Hot Tropics Sipper

4 cups pineapple juice
2 cups apple juice
1 container (11.3 ounces) apricot nectar (1⅓ cups)
½ cup packed dark brown sugar
1 medium lemon, thinly sliced
1 medium orange, thinly sliced
3 whole cinnamon sticks
6 whole cloves
   Additional orange and lemon slices (optional)

1. Place juices, nectar, brown sugar, lemon, orange, cinnamon and cloves in slow cooker. Cover; cook on HIGH 3½ to 4 hours or until very fragrant.

2. Strain immediately (beverage will turn bitter if fruit and spices remain after cooking is complete). Garnish with orange and lemon slices.   *Makes 8 servings*

Prep Time: 5 minutes
Cook Time: 3½ to 4 hours (HIGH)

Steamed Southern Sweet Potato Custard

1 can (16 ounces) cut sweet potatoes, drained
1 can (12 ounces) evaporated milk, divided
½ cup packed light brown sugar
2 eggs, lightly beaten
1 teaspoon ground cinnamon
½ teaspoon ground ginger
¼ teaspoon salt
   Whipped cream (optional)
   Ground nutmeg (optional)

1. Process sweet potatoes and ¼ cup evaporated milk in food processor or blender until smooth. Add remaining milk, brown sugar, eggs, cinnamon, ginger and salt; process until well blended. Pour into ungreased 1-quart soufflé dish. Cover tightly with foil. Crumple large sheet of foil (about 15×12 inches); place in bottom of slow cooker. Pour 2 cups water over foil. Make foil handles.*

2. Transfer dish to slow cooker using foil handles. Cover; cook on HIGH 2½ to 3 hours or until skewer inserted into center comes out clean.

3. Use foil handles to lift dish from slow cooker; transfer to wire rack. Uncover; let stand 30 minutes. Garnish with whipped cream and nutmeg. *Makes 4 servings*

*To make foil handles, tear off 3 (18×3-inch) strips of heavy-duty foil. Crisscross the strips so they resemble the spokes of a wheel. Place the dish in the center of the strips. Pull the foil strips up and over the dish and place it into the slow cooker. Leave the foil strips in while the food cooks, so you can easily lift the item out again when it is finished cooking.

Mixed Berry Cobbler

    1 package (16 ounces) frozen mixed berries
    ¾ cup granulated sugar
    2 tablespoons quick-cooking tapioca
    2 teaspoons grated lemon peel
   1½ cups all-purpose flour
    ½ cup packed brown sugar
  2¼ teaspoons baking powder
    ¼ teaspoon ground nutmeg
    ¾ cup milk
    ⅓ cup butter, melted
    Ice cream (optional)

1. Stir together frozen berries, granulated sugar, tapioca and lemon peel in slow cooker.

2. Combine flour, brown sugar, baking powder and nutmeg in medium bowl. Add milk and butter; stir just until blended. Drop spoonfuls of dough on top of berry mixture.

3. Cover; cook on LOW 4 hours. Uncover; let stand about 30 minutes. Serve with ice cream, if desired.   *Makes 8 servings*

Prep Time: 10 minutes
Cook Time: 4 hours (LOW)
Stand Time: 30 minutes

Gingered Pineapple and Cranberries

2 cans (20 ounces each) pineapple chunks in juice, undrained
1 cup dried sweetened cranberries
½ cup packed brown sugar
1 teaspoon curry powder, divided
1 teaspoon grated fresh ginger, divided
¼ teaspoon red pepper flakes
2 tablespoons water
1 tablespoon cornstarch

1. Place pineapple with juice, cranberries, brown sugar, ½ teaspoon curry powder, ½ teaspoon ginger and red pepper flakes in 1½-quart slow cooker. Cover; cook on HIGH 3 hours.

2. Combine water, cornstarch, remaining ½ teaspoon curry powder and ½ teaspoon ginger in small bowl; stir until cornstarch is dissolved. Add to pineapple mixture. Cook, uncovered, on HIGH 15 minutes or until thickened.   *Makes 4½ cups*

Variation: Substitute 2 cans (20 ounces each) pineapple tidbits in heavy syrup for pineapple and brown sugar.

Pecan-Cinnamon Pudding Cake

1⅓ cups all-purpose flour
½ cup granulated sugar
1½ teaspoons baking powder
1½ teaspoons ground cinnamon
⅔ cup milk
5 tablespoons butter, melted, divided
1 cup chopped pecans
1½ cups water
¾ cup packed brown sugar
Whipped cream (optional)

1. Stir together flour, granulated sugar, baking powder and cinnamon in medium bowl. Add milk and 3 tablespoons butter; mix just until blended. Stir in pecans. Spread on bottom of slow cooker.

2. Combine water, brown sugar and remaining 2 tablespoons butter in small saucepan; bring to a boil. Pour over batter in slow cooker.

3. Cover; cook on HIGH 1¼ to 1½ hours or until toothpick inserted into center comes out clean. Let stand, uncovered, 30 minutes. Serve warm with whipped cream, if desired. *Makes 8 servings*

Prep Time: 20 minutes
Cook Time: 1¼ to 1½ hours (HIGH)
Stand Time: 30 minutes

The publisher would like to thank the companies listed below for the use of their recipes and photographs in this publication.

Campbell Soup Company

ConAgra Foods, Inc.

Recipes to Share Notes

Asian Barbecue Skewers

Sun-Dried Tomato Appetizer Torte

2 pounds boneless skinless chicken
   thighs
½ cup soy sauce
⅓ cup packed brown sugar
2 tablespoons sesame oil
3 cloves garlic, minced
½ cup thinly sliced green onions
   (optional)
1 tablespoon toasted sesame seeds

1. Cut each thigh into 4 pieces about 1½ inches thick. Thread chicken onto 7-inch wooden skewers, folding thinner pieces, if necessary. Place skewers in 6-quart slow cooker, layering as flat as possible.

2. Combine soy sauce, brown sugar, oil and garlic in small bowl. Reserve ⅓ cup sauce; set aside. Pour remaining sauce over skewers. Cover; cook on LOW 2 hours. Turn skewers over; cook 1 hour longer.

3. Transfer skewers to serving platter. Discard cooking liquid. Pour reserved sauce over skewers; sprinkle with green onions, if desired, and sesame seeds.

Makes 4 to 6 servings

Prep Time: 10 minutes
Cook Time: 3 hours (LOW)

---

3 cups chopped onion
3 jars (about 7 ounces each)
   oil-packed sun-dried tomatoes,
   drained and finely chopped
3 tablespoons sugar
1 tablespoon minced garlic
1 piece (2 inches) fresh ginger, peeled
   and grated
1 teaspoon herbes de Provence
½ teaspoon salt
½ cup red wine vinegar
1 package (8 ounces) cream cheese
   Fresh basil sprigs (optional)
   Assorted crackers

1. Place onion, tomatoes, sugar, garlic, ginger, herbes de Provence and salt in slow cooker. Pour in red wine vinegar; stir gently to mix. Cover; cook on LOW 4 to 5 hours or on HIGH 3 hours, stirring occasionally. Let mixture cool before using.

2. To serve, slice cream cheese in half horizontally (use dental floss for clean cut). Spread ⅓ cup tomato mixture onto one cream cheese half. Top with second cream cheese half and spread ⅓ cup tomato mixture on top. Garnish with fresh basil sprigs and serve with crackers. Refrigerate or freeze remaining tomato mixture for another use.

Makes 8 servings

Prep Time: 10 minutes
Cook Time: 4 to 5 hours (LOW) or 3 hours (HIGH)

Tip: Use leftover tomato mixture as a topping for bruschetta or toss with hot cooked pasta.

Steamed Pork Buns

Caponata

½ container (18 ounces) refrigerated shredded cooked pork in barbecue sauce*

1 tablespoon Asian garlic chili sauce

1 package (about 16 ounces) refrigerated biscuit dough (8 large biscuits)

Dipping Sauce (recipe follows)

Sliced green onions (optional)

*Look for pork in plain, not smoky, barbecue sauce. Substitute chicken in barbecue sauce, if desired.

1. Combine pork and chili sauce in medium bowl. Split biscuits in half. Roll or stretch each biscuit into 4-inch circle. Spoon 1 tablespoon pork onto center of each biscuit. Gather edges around filling and press to seal.

2. Generously butter 2-quart baking dish that fits inside 5- or 6-quart slow cooker. Arrange filled biscuits in single layer, overlapping slightly if necessary. Cover dish with buttered foil, buttered side down.

3. Place small rack in slow cooker. Add 1 inch hot water (water should not come to top of rack). Place baking dish on rack. Cover; cook on HIGH 2 hours.

4. Meanwhile, prepare Dipping Sauce. Garnish pork buns with green onions. Serve with Dipping Sauce.   *Makes 8 servings*

Dipping Sauce: Stir together 2 tablespoons rice vinegar, 2 tablespoons soy sauce, 4 teaspoons sugar and 1 teaspoon toasted sesame oil in a small bowl until sugar dissolves. Sprinkle with 1 tablespoon minced green onion (green part only) just before serving.

---

1 medium eggplant (about 1 pound), peeled and cut into ½-inch pieces

1 can (about 14 ounces) diced Italian plum tomatoes

1 medium onion, chopped

1 red bell pepper, cut into ½-inch pieces

½ cup salsa

¼ cup olive oil

2 tablespoons capers, drained

2 tablespoons balsamic vinegar

3 cloves garlic, minced

1 teaspoon dried oregano

¼ teaspoon salt

⅓ cup packed fresh basil, cut into thin strips

Toasted Italian or French bread slices

1. Combine eggplant, tomatoes, onion, bell pepper, salsa, oil, capers, vinegar, garlic, oregano and salt in slow cooker. Cover; cook on LOW 7 to 8 hours or until vegetables are crisp-tender.

2. Stir in basil. Serve at room temperature on toasted bread.   *Makes about 5¼ cups*

Tip: Be sure to cut all of the ingredients for the Caponata into uniform pieces. This allows them to cook evenly in the slow cooker.

Swiss Cheese Fondue

Honey-Mustard Chicken Wings

1 clove garlic, cut in half
1 can (10½ ounces) CAMPBELL'S®
    Condensed Chicken Broth
2 cans (10¾ ounces each)
    CAMPBELL'S® Condensed
    Cheddar Cheese Soup
1 cup water
½ cup Chablis or other dry white
    wine
1 tablespoon Dijon-style mustard
1 tablespoon cornstarch
1 pound shredded Emmentaler
    or Gruyère cheese, at room
    temperature
¼ teaspoon ground nutmeg
    Dash ground black pepper
    PEPPERIDGE FARM® Garlic
    Bread, baked and cut into cubes
    Fresh vegetables for dipping

1. Rub the inside of a 5½- to 6-quart slow cooker with the cut sides of the garlic. Discard the garlic. Stir the broth, soup, water, wine, mustard, cornstarch, cheese, nutmeg and black pepper in the cooker.

2. Cover and cook on LOW for 1 hour or until the cheese is melted, stirring occasionally.

3. Serve with the bread and vegetables on skewers for dipping.   *Makes 6 servings*

Prep Time: 10 minutes
Cook Time: 1 hour

CAMPBELL'S® Kitchen Tip: This recipe may be doubled.

---

3 pounds chicken wings
1 teaspoon salt
1 teaspoon black pepper
½ cup honey
½ cup barbecue sauce
2 tablespoons spicy brown mustard
1 clove garlic, minced
3 to 4 thin lemon slices

1. Cut off chicken wing tips; discard. Cut each wing at joint to make two pieces. Sprinkle with salt and pepper; place wing pieces on broiler rack. Broil 4 to 5 inches from heat about 10 minutes, turning halfway through cooking time. Place in slow cooker.

2. Combine honey, barbecue sauce, mustard and garlic in small bowl; mix well. Pour sauce over chicken wings. Top with lemon slices. Cover; cook on LOW 4 to 5 hours.

3. Remove and discard lemon slices. Serve wings with sauce from slow cooker.
                                                          Makes about 24 wings

Prep Time: 20 minutes
Cook Time: 4 to 5 hours (LOW)

Tip: Browning the chicken wings in the broiler before cooking them in the slow cooker is not necessary, but will enhance their flavor and appearance.

Easy Party Meatballs

Spicy, Sweet & Sour Cocktail Franks

1 jar (1 pound 10 ounces) PREGO®
    Marinara Italian Sauce
1 jar (12 ounces) grape jelly

½ cup prepared chili sauce
2½ pounds frozen fully-cooked
    meatballs, cocktail size

1. Stir the Italian sauce, jelly, chili sauce and meatballs in a 4½-quart slow cooker.

2. Cover and cook on LOW for 6 to 7 hours* or until the meatballs are cooked through. Serve the meatballs on a serving plate with toothpicks.   *Makes 8 servings*

*Or on HIGH for 3 to 4 hours.

Prep Time: 5 minutes
Cook Time: 6 to 7 hours

CAMPBELL'S® Kitchen Tips: Larger-size or turkey meatballs can also be used, if desired. For a special touch, serve with cranberry chutney for dipping.

2 packages (8 ounces each) cocktail
    franks
½ cup ketchup or chili sauce
½ cup apricot preserves

1 teaspoon hot pepper sauce
Additional hot pepper sauce
    (optional)

1. Combine all ingredients in 1½-quart slow cooker; mix well. Cover; cook on LOW 2 to 3 hours.

2. Serve warm or at room temperature with additional hot pepper sauce, if desired.
                              Makes about 4 dozen cocktail franks

Prep Time: 8 minutes
Cook Time: 2 to 3 hours (LOW)

Tomato Topping for Bruschetta

Brats in Beer

3 medium tomatoes, peeled, cored, seeded and diced
1 stalk celery, chopped
1 shallot, chopped
2 pepperoncini peppers, chopped*
1 teaspoon tomato paste
½ teaspoon salt
¼ teaspoon black pepper
1 tablespoon olive oil
4 large slices Italian or French bread
1 clove garlic

Pepperoncini are pickled peppers sold in jars with brine. They are available in the condiment aisle of the supermarket.

1. Drain any tomato juices. Combine tomatoes, celery, shallot, pepperoncini peppers, tomato paste, salt, black pepper and oil in slow cooker. Cover; cook on LOW 45 minutes to 1 hour.

2. Toast bread. Immediately rub with garlic. Spread tomato topping on bread. Serve immediately.   *Makes 4 servings*

Prep Time: 10 minutes
Cook Time: 45 minutes to 1 hour (LOW)

1½ pounds bratwurst (about 5 or 6 links)
1 bottle (12 ounces) amber ale
1 medium onion, thinly sliced
2 tablespoons packed brown sugar
2 tablespoons red wine vinegar or cider vinegar
Spicy brown mustard
Cocktail rye bread

1. Combine bratwurst, ale, onion, brown sugar and vinegar in slow cooker. Cover; cook on LOW 4 to 5 hours.

2. Remove bratwurst and onion slices from slow cooker. Cut bratwurst into ½-inch-thick slices. For mini open-faced sandwiches, spread mustard on cocktail rye bread. Top with bratwurst slices and onion.   *Makes 30 to 36 appetizers*

Prep Time: 5 minutes
Cook Time: 4 to 5 hours

Tip: Choose a light-tasting beer for cooking brats. Hearty ales can leave the meat tasting slightly bitter.

Simmering Hot & Sour Soup

Burgundy Beef Po' Boys with Dipping Sauce

2 cans (about 14 ounces each) chicken broth

1 cup chopped cooked chicken or pork

4 ounces fresh shiitake mushroom caps, thinly sliced

½ cup sliced bamboo shoots, cut into thin strips

3 tablespoons rice wine vinegar

2 tablespoons soy sauce

1½ teaspoons Chinese chili paste *or* 1 teaspoon hot chili oil

4 ounces firm tofu, well drained and cut into ½-inch pieces

2 teaspoons dark sesame oil

2 tablespoons cornstarch

2 tablespoons cold water

Chopped cilantro or sliced green onions (optional)

1. Combine broth, chicken, mushrooms, bamboo shoots, vinegar, soy sauce and chili paste in slow cooker. Cover; cook on LOW 3 to 4 hours.

2. Stir in tofu and sesame oil. Blend cornstarch and water in small bowl until smooth. Stir into slow cooker. Cover; cook on HIGH 15 minutes or until soup is thickened.

3. Serve hot; garnish with cilantro.   *Makes 4 servings*

---

1 boneless beef chuck shoulder or bottom round roast (3 pounds)

2 cups chopped onions

¼ cup red wine

3 tablespoons balsamic vinegar

1 tablespoon beef bouillon granules

1 tablespoon Worcestershire sauce

¾ teaspoon dried thyme

½ teaspoon garlic powder

Italian rolls, warmed and split

1. Cut beef into 3 or 4 pieces; trim fat. Place onions in slow cooker. Top with beef, wine, vinegar, bouillon, Worcestershire, thyme and garlic powder. Cover; cook on HIGH 8 to 10 hours or until beef is very tender.

2. Remove beef; cool slightly and remove excess fat. Shred with two forks.

3. Let cooking liquid stand 5 minutes. Skim off fat. Serve beef on rolls. Serve with cooking liquid as dipping sauce.   *Makes 6 to 8 sandwiches*

Mediterranean Shrimp Soup

Hot Beef Sandwiches

2 cans (about 14 ounces each) chicken broth
1 can (about 14 ounces) diced tomatoes
1 can (8 ounces) tomato sauce
1 medium onion, chopped
½ medium green bell pepper, chopped
½ cup orange juice
½ cup dry white wine (optional)

1 jar (2½ ounces) sliced mushrooms
¼ cup sliced pitted black olives
2 cloves garlic, minced
1 teaspoon dried basil
2 bay leaves
¼ teaspoon whole fennel seeds, crushed
⅛ teaspoon black pepper
1 pound medium raw shrimp, peeled and deveined

1. Place all ingredients except shrimp in slow cooker. Cover; cook on LOW 4 to 4½ hours or until vegetables are crisp-tender.

2. Stir in shrimp. Cover; cook 15 to 30 minutes or until shrimp are pink and opaque. Remove and discard bay leaves. *Makes 6 servings*

Tip: For a heartier soup, add 1 pound of firm white fish, such as cod or haddock, cut into 1-inch pieces. Add the fish to the slow cooker 45 minutes before serving. Cook, covered, on LOW.

---

1 beef chuck roast (3 to 4 pounds), cut into chunks
1 jar (6 ounces) sliced dill pickles, undrained
1 can (about 14 ounces) crushed tomatoes with Italian seasoning

1 medium onion, diced
4 cloves garlic, minced
1 teaspoon mustard seeds
Hamburger buns

1. Place beef in slow cooker. Pour pickles with juice over beef. Add tomatoes, onion, garlic and mustard seeds.

2. Cover; cook on LOW 8 to 10 hours.

3. Remove beef from slow cooker. Shred beef with two forks. Return beef to tomato mixture; mix well. Serve beef mixture on buns. *Makes 6 to 8 servings*

Serving Suggestion: Garnish with lettuce, sliced tomatoes, red onion slices, shredded slaw or other fixings to taste.

Fennel Soup au Gratin

Tavern Burger

8 cups SWANSON® Beef Broth (Regular, 50% Less Sodium or Certified Organic)

2 tablespoons dry sherry

2 teaspoons dried thyme leaves, crushed

3 tablespoons butter

1 bulb fennel, sliced (about 4 cups)

2 medium onions, sliced (about 4 cups)

8 ounces French bread, sliced ½-inch thick

½ cup shredded Italian blend cheese

1. Stir the broth, sherry, thyme, butter, fennel and onions in a 5½-quart slow cooker. Cover and cook on HIGH for 6 hours.

2. Just before serving, top **each** bread slice with **1 tablespoon** of the cheese. Place the bread on a baking sheet. Broil 4 inches from the heat for 1 minute or until golden.

3. Divide the soup mixture among **8** serving bowls. Top **each** serving of soup with a cheese toast. *Makes 8 servings*

Prep Time: 15 minutes
Cook Time: 6 hours

2 pounds 95% lean ground beef

½ cup ketchup

¼ cup packed brown sugar

¼ cup yellow mustard

Hamburger buns

1. Brown beef 6 to 8 minutes in medium skillet over medium-high heat, stirring to break up meat. Drain fat. Transfer beef to slow cooker.

2. Add ketchup, brown sugar and mustard to slow cooker; mix well. Cover; cook on LOW 4 to 6 hours. Serve on buns. *Makes 8 servings*

Variation: For added flavor, add a can of pork and beans with the beef.

Fiesta Black Bean Soup

Italian Beef and Barley Soup

6 cups chicken broth
12 ounces potatoes, peeled and diced
1 can (about 15 ounces) black beans, rinsed and drained
½ pound cooked ham, diced
½ onion, diced
1 can (4 ounces) chopped jalapeño peppers
2 cloves garlic, minced
2 teaspoons dried oregano
1½ teaspoons dried thyme
1 teaspoon ground cumin
Toppings: sour cream, chopped bell pepper and chopped tomatoes (optional)

1. Combine broth, potatoes, beans, ham, onion, jalapeños, garlic, oregano, thyme and cumin in slow cooker; mix well.

2. Cover; cook on LOW 8 to 10 hours or on HIGH 4 to 5 hours.

3. Adjust seasonings. Serve with desired toppings.   *Makes 6 to 8 servings*

1 boneless beef top sirloin steak (about 1½ pounds)
1 tablespoon vegetable oil
4 medium carrots or parsnips, cut into ¼-inch slices
1 cup chopped onion
1 teaspoon dried thyme
½ teaspoon dried rosemary
¼ teaspoon black pepper
⅓ cup uncooked pearl barley
2 cans (about 14 ounces each) beef broth
1 can (about 14 ounces) diced tomatoes with Italian seasoning

1. Cut beef into 1-inch pieces. Heat oil over medium-high heat in large skillet. Brown beef on all sides; set aside.

2. Place carrots and onion in slow cooker; sprinkle with thyme, rosemary and pepper. Top with barley and beef. Pour broth and tomatoes over beef.

3. Cover; cook on LOW 8 to 10 hours or until beef is tender.   *Makes 6 servings*

Prep Time: 20 minutes
Cook Time: 8 to 10 hours (LOW)

Tip: Choose pearl barley rather than quick-cooking barley, because it will stand up to longer cooking.

Hot & Juicy Reuben Sandwiches

Slow-Cooked Pulled Pork Sandwiches

1 mild-cure corned beef (about
  1½ pounds)
2 cups sauerkraut, drained
½ cup beef broth
1 small onion, sliced
1 clove garlic, minced

¼ teaspoon caraway seeds
4 to 6 peppercorns
8 slices pumpernickel or rye bread
4 slices Swiss cheese
  Mustard

1. Trim excess fat from corned beef. Place beef in slow cooker. Add sauerkraut, broth, onion, garlic, caraway seeds and peppercorns.

2. Cover; cook on LOW 7 to 9 hours.

3. Remove beef from slow cooker. Cut across the grain into ¼-inch-thick slices. Divide evenly among 4 slices of bread. Top each slice with ½ cup drained sauerkraut mixture and 1 slice of cheese. Spread mustard on remaining 4 bread slices. Close sandwiches.

Makes 4 servings

Prep Time: 25 minutes
Cook Time: 7 to 9 hours (LOW)

---

1 tablespoon vegetable oil
1 (3½- to 4-pound) boneless pork
  shoulder roast, netted or tied
1 can (10½ ounces) CAMPBELL'S®
  Condensed French Onion Soup

 1 cup ketchup
¼ cup cider vinegar
 3 tablespoons packed brown sugar
12 round sandwich rolls, split

1. Heat the oil in a 10-inch skillet over medium-high heat. Add the roast and cook until it's well browned on all sides.

2. Stir the soup, ketchup, vinegar and brown sugar in a 5-quart slow cooker. Add the roast and turn to coat with the soup mixture.

3. Cover and cook on LOW for 8 to 10 hours* or until the meat is fork-tender.

4. Remove the roast from the cooker to a cutting board and let it stand for 10 minutes. Using 2 forks, shred the pork. Return the shredded pork to the cooker.

5. Divide the pork and sauce mixture among the rolls. *Makes 12 sandwiches*

*Or on HIGH for 4 to 5 hours.

Start to Finish Time: 8 to 10 hours, 25 minutes
Prepping: 15 minutes
Cooking: 8 to 10 hours
Standing: 10 minutes

Lemon Pork Chops

Forty-Clove Chicken

1 tablespoon vegetable oil
4 boneless pork chops
3 cans (8 ounces each) tomato sauce
1 large onion, quartered and sliced (optional)
1 large green bell pepper, cut into strips

1 tablespoon lemon-pepper seasoning
1 tablespoon Worcestershire sauce
1 lemon, quartered
Lemon wedges (optional)

1. Heat oil in large skillet over medium heat. Brown pork chops on both sides. Drain fat. Transfer pork chops to slow cooker.

2. Combine tomato sauce, onion, if desired, bell pepper, lemon-pepper seasoning and Worcestershire sauce in medium bowl. Add to slow cooker.

3. Squeeze juice from lemon quarters over mixture; place squeezed lemon quarters in slow cooker. Cover; cook on LOW 6 to 8 hours or until pork is tender. Remove lemon wedges before serving. Garnish with additional lemon wedges.   *Makes 4 servings*

Prep Time: 10 minutes
Cook Time: 6 to 8 hours (LOW)

Serving Suggestions: Great served with green beans and couscous.

---

1 whole chicken (3 pounds), cut up
  Salt and black pepper
1 to 2 tablespoons olive oil
¼ cup dry white wine
2 tablespoons chopped fresh parsley
  or 2 teaspoons dried parsley
2 tablespoons dry vermouth

2 teaspoons dried basil
1 teaspoon dried oregano
  Pinch red pepper flakes
40 cloves garlic (about 2 bulbs), peeled
4 stalks celery, sliced
  Juice and peel of 1 lemon

1. Remove skin from chicken. Sprinkle chicken with salt and pepper. Heat oil in large skillet over medium heat. Add chicken; brown on all sides. Remove to platter.

2. Combine wine, parsley, vermouth, basil, oregano and red pepper flakes in large bowl. Add garlic and celery; coat well. Transfer garlic and celery to slow cooker with slotted spoon. Add chicken to remaining herb mixture; coat well. Place chicken on top of celery mixture in slow cooker. Sprinkle lemon juice and peel over chicken. Cover; cook on LOW 6 hours.   *Makes 4 to 6 servings*

Curry Beef

Italian Meatballs & Peppers

1 pound 90% lean ground beef
1 medium onion, thinly sliced
½ cup beef broth
1 tablespoon curry powder
1 teaspoon ground cumin
2 cloves garlic, minced
1 cup sour cream
¼ cup milk

½ cup raisins, divided
1 teaspoon sugar
12 ounces uncooked wide egg noodles
    or 1⅓ cups uncooked long grain white rice
¼ cup chopped walnuts, almonds or pecans

1. Brown beef 6 to 8 minutes in large skillet over medium-high heat, stirring to break up meat. Drain fat. Combine beef, onion, broth, curry powder, cumin and garlic in slow cooker. Cover; cook on LOW 4 hours.

2. Stir in sour cream, milk, ¼ cup raisins and sugar. Cover; cook 30 minutes or until thickened and heated through.

3. Cook noodles according to package directions; drain. Spoon beef curry over noodles. Sprinkle with remaining ¼ cup raisins and walnuts. *Makes 4 servings*

Serving Suggestion: Serve with sliced cucumber sprinkled with sugar and vinegar or plain yogurt topped with brown sugar, chopped bananas and green onions.

---

2 cans (28 ounces each) HUNT'S®
    Diced Tomatoes with Basil,
    Garlic & Oregano, undrained
1 can (6 ounces) HUNT'S® Tomato
    Paste

1 package (16 ounces) frozen cooked
    meatballs
1 package (14 ounces) frozen bell
    pepper strips

1. Combine tomatoes, tomato paste, meatballs and pepper strips in slow cooker.

2. Cook on LOW setting for 8 to 10 hours or on HIGH setting for 4 to 6 hours.
 Makes 8 servings (1 cup each with 4 meatballs)

Prep Time: 10 minutes
Total Time: 8 hours

Harvest Ham Supper

Fiery Chili Beef

6 carrots, cut into 2-inch pieces
3 medium sweet potatoes, quartered

1 to 1½ pounds boneless ham
1 cup maple syrup

1. Place carrots and potatoes in bottom of slow cooker. Place ham on top of vegetables. Pour syrup over ham and vegetables.

2. Cover; cook on LOW 6 to 8 hours.

Makes 6 servings

Prep Time: 10 minutes
Cook Time: 6 to 8 hours (LOW)

1 to 2 beef flank steaks (1 to 1½ pounds)
1 can (28 ounces) diced tomatoes
1 can (15 ounces) pinto beans, rinsed and drained
1 medium onion, chopped
2 cloves garlic, minced
½ teaspoon salt

½ teaspoon ground cumin
¼ teaspoon black pepper
1 canned chipotle chile pepper in adobo sauce
1 teaspoon adobo sauce from canned chile pepper
Flour tortillas (optional)

1. Cut flank steak into 6 equal pieces. Combine flank steak, tomatoes, beans, onion, garlic, salt, cumin and black pepper in slow cooker.

2. Dice chile pepper. Add pepper and adobo sauce to slow cooker; mix well.

3. Cover; cook on LOW 7 to 8 hours. Serve with tortillas, if desired.

Makes 6 servings

Prep Time: 15 minutes
Cook Time: 7 to 8 hours (LOW)

Tip: Chipotle chile peppers are dried, smoked jalapeño peppers with a very hot yet smoky, sweet flavor. They can be found dried, pickled and canned in adobo sauce.

Southwestern Stuffed Peppers

Chicken Cacciatore

4 green bell peppers

1 can (about 15 ounces) black beans, rinsed and drained

1 cup (4 ounces) shredded pepper jack cheese

¾ cup salsa

½ cup frozen corn

½ cup chopped green onions

⅓ cup uncooked long grain converted white rice

1 teaspoon chili powder

½ teaspoon ground cumin

Sour cream (optional)

1. Cut thin slice off top of each bell pepper. Carefully remove seeds, leaving peppers whole.

2. Combine beans, cheese, salsa, corn, green onions, rice, chili powder and cumin in medium bowl. Spoon filling evenly into peppers. Place peppers in slow cooker. Cover; cook on LOW 4 to 6 hours. Serve with sour cream, if desired.   *Makes 4 servings*

Prep Time: 15 minutes
Cook Time: 4 to 6 hours (LOW)

1½ cups SWANSON® Chicken Stock

2 teaspoons garlic powder

2 cans (14½ ounces each) diced Italian-style tomatoes

4 cups mushrooms, cut in half (about 12 ounces)

2 large onions, chopped (about 2 cups)

3 pounds chicken parts, skin removed

¼ cup cornstarch

10 cups hot cooked spaghetti

1. Stir **1 cup** stock, garlic powder, tomatoes, mushrooms and onions in a 5- to 6-quart slow cooker. Add the chicken and turn to coat.

2. Cover and cook on LOW for 7 to 8 hours* or until the chicken is cooked through. Remove the chicken from the cooker and keep warm.

3. Stir the cornstarch and remaining stock in a small bowl until the mixture is smooth. Stir the cornstarch mixture in the cooker. Cover and cook on HIGH for 10 minutes or until the mixture boils and thickens. Serve with the chicken and spaghetti.

Makes 6 servings

*Or on HIGH for 4 to 5 hours.

Prep Time: 10 minutes
Cook Time: 8 hours

Serving Suggestions: Serve with a tomato and cucumber salad with fresh basil and Italian viniagrette. For dessert serve almond biscotti.

Sweet 'n' Spicy Ribs

Beef and Vegetables in Rich Burgundy Sauce

5 cups barbecue sauce
¾ cup packed brown sugar
¼ cup honey
2 tablespoons Cajun seasoning
1 tablespoon garlic powder

1 tablespoon onion powder
6 pounds pork or beef back ribs,
    cut into 3-rib or individual rib
    portions

1. Stir together barbecue sauce, brown sugar, honey, Cajun seasoning, garlic powder and onion powder in medium bowl. Reserve 1 cup mixture for dipping sauce; refrigerate until ready to serve.

2. Place ribs in slow cooker. Pour remaining barbecue sauce mixture over ribs. Cover; cook on LOW 8 hours or until meat is very tender.

3. Serve ribs with reserved sauce. *Makes 10 servings*

Prep Time: 10 to 15 minutes
Cook Time: 8 hours (LOW)

Tip: To make the slow cooker cleanup easier, spray the inside with nonstick cooking spray before adding any of the ingredients.

---

1 package (8 ounces) baby carrots
1 package (8 ounces) sliced
    mushrooms
1 medium green bell pepper, cut into
    thin strips
1 boneless beef chuck roast
    (2½ pounds)
1 can (10¾ ounces) condensed
    golden mushroom soup,
    undiluted

¼ cup dry red wine or beef broth
1 package (1 ounce) dry onion soup
    mix
1 tablespoon Worcestershire sauce
¼ teaspoon black pepper
3 tablespoons cornstarch
2 tablespoons water
4 cups hot cooked noodles
    Chopped fresh parsley (optional)

1. Place carrots, mushrooms and bell pepper in slow cooker. Place roast on top of vegetables. Combine mushroom soup, wine, soup mix, Worcestershire sauce and black pepper in medium bowl; mix well. Pour soup mixture over roast. Cover; cook on LOW 8 to 10 hours.

2. Transfer roast to cutting board; cover with foil. Let stand 10 to 15 minutes before slicing.

3. Blend cornstarch and water until smooth; stir into slow cooker. Cook, uncovered, 15 minutes or until thickened. Serve beef and vegetables with sauce over cooked noodles. Garnish with parsley. *Makes 6 to 8 servings*

Barley with Currants and Pine Nuts

Rustic Cheddar Mashed Potatoes

1 tablespoon butter
1 small onion, finely chopped
2 cups chicken or vegetable broth
½ cup pearled barley

½ teaspoon salt
¼ teaspoon black pepper
⅓ cup currants
¼ cup pine nuts

1. Melt butter in small skillet over medium-high heat. Add onion. Cook and stir 2 minutes or until lightly browned. Transfer to slow cooker. Add broth, barley, salt and pepper. Stir in currants. Cover; cook on LOW 3 hours.

2. Stir in pine nuts; serve immediately.   *Makes 4 servings*

Prep Time: 10 minutes
Cook Time: 3 hours (LOW)

2 pounds russet potatoes, peeled and
    diced
1 cup water
⅓ cup butter, cut into small pieces
½ to ¾ cup milk

1¼ teaspoons salt
½ teaspoon black pepper
½ cup finely chopped green onions
¾ cup (3 ounces) shredded Cheddar
    cheese

1. Combine potatoes and water in slow cooker; dot with butter. Cover; cook on LOW 6 hours or on HIGH 3 hours or until potatoes are tender. Remove potatoes to large mixing bowl.

2. Beat potatoes with electric mixer at medium speed until fluffy. Add milk, salt and pepper; beat until smooth.

3. Stir in green onions and cheese; cover. Let stand 15 minutes to allow flavors to blend and cheese to melt.   *Makes 8 servings*

Tip: To easily and thoroughly dot the potatoes with butter, grate cold butter with the large holes of a box grater directly over the potatoes.

Five-Bean Casserole

Spinach Spoon Bread

2 medium onions, chopped
8 ounces bacon, diced
2 cloves garlic, minced
½ cup packed brown sugar
½ cup cider vinegar
1 teaspoon salt
1 teaspoon dry mustard
¼ teaspoon black pepper
2 cans (about 15 ounces each) kidney
    beans, rinsed and drained

1 can (about 15 ounces) chickpeas,
    rinsed and drained
1 can (about 15 ounces) butter beans,
    rinsed and drained
1 can (about 15 ounces) Great
    Northern or cannellini beans,
    rinsed and drained
1 can (about 15 ounces) baked beans

1. Cook and stir onions, bacon and garlic in large skillet over medium heat until onions are tender; drain. Stir in brown sugar, vinegar, salt, mustard and pepper. Simmer over low heat 15 minutes.

2. Combine beans in slow cooker. Spoon onion mixture evenly over top. Cover; cook on LOW 6 to 8 hours or on HIGH 3 to 4 hours.   *Makes 16 servings*

---

1 package (10 ounces) frozen
    chopped spinach, thawed and
    squeezed dry
1 red bell pepper, diced
4 eggs, lightly beaten
1 cup cottage cheese

1 package (5½ ounces) cornbread mix
6 green onions, sliced
½ cup (1 stick) butter, melted
1¼ teaspoons seasoned salt

1. Lightly grease slow cooker. Turn heat to HIGH.

2. Combine all ingredients in large bowl; mix well. Pour batter into prepared slow cooker. Place lid on slow cooker slightly ajar to allow excess moisture to escape. Cook on LOW 3 to 4 hours or on HIGH 1¾ to 2 hours or until edges are golden and knife inserted into center of bread comes out clean.

3. To serve, scoop bread from slow cooker with spoon. Or, loosen edges and bottom with knife and invert onto plate; cut into wedges.   *Makes 8 servings*

Tip: Spoon bread is a soft, moist egg-based dish made with cornmeal and sometimes corn kernels. It is more like a pudding than a bread and, as its name indicates, can be served with a spoon.

Scalloped Potatoes

Cheesy Corn and Peppers

Vegetable cooking spray

3 pounds Yukon Gold or Eastern
potatoes, thinly sliced (about
9 cups)

1 large onion, thinly sliced (about
1 cup)

1 can (10¾ ounces) CAMPBELL'S®
Condensed Cream of
Mushroom Soup (Regular, 98%
Fat Free or 25% Less Sodium)

½ cup CAMPBELL'S® Condensed
Chicken Broth

1 cup shredded Cheddar or crumbled
blue cheese (about 4 ounces)

1. Spray the inside of a 6-quart slow cooker with the cooking spray. Layer a third of the potatoes and half of the onion in the cooker. Repeat the layers. Top with the remaining potatoes.

2. Stir the soup and broth in a small bowl. Pour over the potatoes. Cover and cook on HIGH for 4 to 5 hours or until the potatoes are tender.

3. Top the potatoes with the cheese. Cover and let stand for 5 minutes or until the cheese is melted.   *Makes 6 servings*

Prep Time: 15 minutes
Cook Time: 4 to 5 hours
Stand Time: 5 minutes

---

2 pounds frozen corn kernels

2 poblano peppers, chopped *or*
1 large green bell pepper and
1 jalapeño pepper,* seeded and
finely chopped

2 tablespoons butter, cubed

1 teaspoon salt

½ teaspoon ground cumin

¼ teaspoon black pepper

1 cup (4 ounces) shredded sharp
Cheddar cheese

3 ounces cream cheese, cubed

*Jalapeño peppers can sting and irritate the skin, so wear rubber gloves when handling peppers and do not touch your eyes. Wash hands after handling.

1. Coat slow cooker with nonstick cooking spray. Add corn, poblanos, butter, salt, cumin and black pepper. Cover; cook on HIGH 2 hours.

2. Add cheeses; stir to blend. Cover; cook 15 minutes more or until cheeses melt.
                                                                Makes 8 servings

Prep Time: 8 minutes
Cook Time: 2¼ hours (HIGH)

Winter Squash and Apples

Risotto-Style Peppered Rice

1 teaspoon salt
½ teaspoon black pepper
1 butternut squash (about 2 pounds),
    peeled and seeded

2 apples, cored and cut into slices
1 medium onion, quartered and
    sliced
2 tablespoons butter

1. Combine salt and pepper in small bowl; set aside.

2. Cut squash into 2-inch pieces; place in slow cooker. Add apples and onion. Sprinkle with salt mixture; stir well. Cover; cook on LOW 6 to 7 hours or until vegetables are tender.

3. Stir in butter just before serving; season to taste with additional salt and pepper.

Makes 4 to 6 servings

Prep Time: 15 minutes
Cook Time: 6 to 7 hours (LOW)

Variation: Add ¼ to ½ cup packed brown sugar and ½ teaspoon ground cinnamon with butter in step 3; mix well. Cook an additional 15 minutes.

---

1 cup uncooked long grain rice
1 green bell pepper, chopped
1 red bell pepper, chopped
1 cup chopped onion
½ teaspoon ground turmeric
⅛ teaspoon ground red pepper
    (optional)

1 can (about 14 ounces) chicken or
    vegetable broth
4 ounces pepper jack cheese, cubed
½ cup milk
¼ cup (½ stick) butter, cubed
1 teaspoon salt

1. Place rice, bell peppers, onions, turmeric and ground red pepper, if desired, in slow cooker. Stir in broth. Cover; cook on LOW 4 to 5 hours.

2. Stir in cheese, milk, butter and salt; fluff rice with fork. Cover; cook on LOW 5 minutes or until cheese melts.

Makes 4 to 6 servings

Lemon-Mint Red Potatoes

Polenta-Style Corn Casserole

2 pounds new red potatoes
3 tablespoons extra-virgin olive oil
¾ teaspoon dried Greek seasoning or
   dried oregano
¼ teaspoon garlic powder
1 teaspoon salt

¼ teaspoon black pepper
1 teaspoon grated lemon peel
2 tablespoons lemon juice
2 tablespoons butter
4 tablespoons chopped fresh mint,
   divided

1. Coat inside of 6-quart slow cooker with nonstick cooking spray. Add potatoes and oil, stirring gently to coat. Sprinkle with Greek seasoning, garlic powder, salt and pepper. Cover; cook on LOW 7 hours or on HIGH 4 hours.

2. Stir in lemon peel, lemon juice, butter and 2 tablespoons mint until butter is completely melted. Cover; cook 15 minutes to allow flavors to blend. Sprinkle with remaining mint. *Makes 4 servings*

Prep Time: 25 minutes
Cook Time: 7¼ hours (LOW) or 4¼ hours (HIGH)

Tip: It's easy to prepare this recipe ahead of time; simply follow instructions as listed and then turn off heat and let stand at room temperature for up to 2 hours. Reheat or serve at room temperature.

---

1 can (about 14 ounces) vegetable or
   chicken broth
½ cup cornmeal
1 can (7 ounces) corn, drained
1 can (4 ounces) diced green chiles,
   drained

¼ cup diced red bell pepper
½ teaspoon salt
¼ teaspoon black pepper
1 cup (4 ounces) shredded Cheddar
   cheese

1. Pour broth into slow cooker. Whisk in cornmeal. Add corn, chiles, bell pepper, salt and pepper. Cover; cook on LOW 4 to 5 hours or on HIGH 2 to 3 hours.

2. Stir in cheese. Cook, uncovered, 15 to 30 minutes or until cheese melts.

Makes 6 servings

Serving Suggestion: Divide cooked corn mixture into lightly greased individual ramekins or spread in pie plate; cover and refrigerate. Serve at room temperature or warm in oven or microwave.

Easy Chocolate Pudding Cake

Cherry Rice Pudding

1 package (6-serving size) instant chocolate pudding and pie filling mix

3 cups milk

1 package (about 18 ounces) chocolate fudge cake mix plus ingredients to prepare mix

Whipped topping or ice cream (optional)

Crushed peppermint candies (optional)

1. Spray 4-quart slow cooker with nonstick cooking spray. Place pudding mix in slow cooker. Whisk in milk.

2. Prepare cake mix according to package directions. Carefully pour cake mix into slow cooker. Do not stir. Cover; cook on HIGH 1½ hours or until cake is set. Serve warm with whipped topping and candies, if desired. *Makes about 16 servings*

Prep Time: 15 minutes
Cook Time: 1½ hours (HIGH)

1½ cups milk

1 cup hot cooked rice

3 eggs, beaten

½ cup sugar

¼ cup dried cherries

½ teaspoon almond extract

¼ teaspoon salt

1. Combine all ingredients in large bowl. Pour mixture into greased 1½-quart casserole. Cover with foil.

2. Place rack in 5-quart slow cooker and pour in 1 cup water. Place casserole on rack. Cover; cook on LOW 4 to 5 hours.

3. Remove casserole from slow cooker. Let stand 15 minutes before serving.

Makes 6 servings

Variation: Try substituting dried cranberries for the dried cherries or add 2 tablespoons of each for a delicious new dish.

Raisin Cinnamon Bread Pudding

Hot Tropics Sipper

Vegetable cooking spray
10 slices PEPPERIDGE FARM®
    Raisin Cinnamon Swirl Bread,
    cut into cubes (about 5 cups)
1 can (14 ounces) sweetened
    condensed milk
1 cup water
1 teaspoon vanilla extract
4 eggs, beaten
    Ice cream (optional)

1. Spray the inside of a 4½- to 5-quart slow cooker with cooking spray.

2. Place the bread in slow cooker.

3. Stir the milk, water, vanilla and eggs with a whisk or fork in a medium bowl. Pour over the bread mixture. Stir and push the bread cubes into milk mixture to coat.

4. Cover and cook on LOW for 2½ to 3 hours or until set. Serve warm with ice cream, if desired.   *Makes 6 servings*

Prep Time: 10 minutes
Cook Time: 2½ to 3 hours

Tip: Even when it's too hot to bake, you can surprise your family with fresh, homemade desserts made in the slow cooker.

---

4 cups pineapple juice
2 cups apple juice
1 container (11.3 ounces) apricot
    nectar (1⅓ cups)
½ cup packed dark brown sugar
1 medium lemon, thinly sliced
1 medium orange, thinly sliced
3 whole cinnamon sticks
6 whole cloves
    Additional orange and lemon slices
    (optional)

1. Place juices, nectar, brown sugar, lemon, orange, cinnamon and cloves in slow cooker. Cover; cook on HIGH 3½ to 4 hours or until very fragrant.

2. Strain immediately (beverage will turn bitter if fruit and spices remain after cooking is complete). Garnish with orange and lemon slices.   *Makes 8 servings*

Prep Time: 5 minutes
Cook Time: 3½ to 4 hours (HIGH)

Steamed Southern Sweet Potato Custard

Mixed Berry Cobbler

1 can (16 ounces) cut sweet potatoes,
　　drained
1 can (12 ounces) evaporated milk,
　　divided
½ cup packed light brown sugar
2 eggs, lightly beaten

1 teaspoon ground cinnamon
½ teaspoon ground ginger
¼ teaspoon salt
　　Whipped cream (optional)
　　Ground nutmeg (optional)

1. Process sweet potatoes and ¼ cup evaporated milk in food processor or blender until smooth. Add remaining milk, brown sugar, eggs, cinnamon, ginger and salt; process until well blended. Pour into ungreased 1-quart soufflé dish. Cover tightly with foil. Crumple large sheet of foil (about 15×12 inches); place in bottom of slow cooker. Pour 2 cups water over foil. Make foil handles.*

2. Transfer dish to slow cooker using foil handles. Cover; cook on HIGH 2½ to 3 hours or until skewer inserted into center comes out clean.

3. Use foil handles to lift dish from slow cooker; transfer to wire rack. Uncover; let stand 30 minutes. Garnish with whipped cream and nutmeg.　　　*Makes 4 servings*

*To make foil handles, tear off 3 (18×3-inch) strips of heavy-duty foil. Crisscross the strips so they resemble the spokes of a wheel. Place the dish in the center of the strips. Pull the foil strips up and over the dish and place it into the slow cooker. Leave the foil strips in while the food cooks, so you can easily lift the item out again when it is finished cooking.

---

1 package (16 ounces) frozen mixed
　　berries
¾ cup granulated sugar
2 tablespoons quick-cooking tapioca
2 teaspoons grated lemon peel
1½ cups all-purpose flour

½ cup packed brown sugar
2¼ teaspoons baking powder
¼ teaspoon ground nutmeg
¾ cup milk
⅓ cup butter, melted
　　Ice cream (optional)

1. Stir together frozen berries, granulated sugar, tapioca and lemon peel in slow cooker.

2. Combine flour, brown sugar, baking powder and nutmeg in medium bowl. Add milk and butter; stir just until blended. Drop spoonfuls of dough on top of berry mixture.

3. Cover; cook on LOW 4 hours. Uncover; let stand about 30 minutes. Serve with ice cream, if desired.　　　*Makes 8 servings*

Prep Time: 10 minutes
Cook Time: 4 hours (LOW)
Stand Time: 30 minutes

Gingered Pineapple and Cranberries

Pecan-Cinnamon Pudding Cake

2 cans (20 ounces each) pineapple
chunks in juice, undrained

1 cup dried sweetened cranberries

½ cup packed brown sugar

1 teaspoon curry powder, divided

1 teaspoon grated fresh ginger,
divided

¼ teaspoon red pepper flakes

2 tablespoons water

1 tablespoon cornstarch

1. Place pineapple with juice, cranberries, brown sugar, ½ teaspoon curry powder,
½ teaspoon ginger and red pepper flakes in 1½-quart slow cooker. Cover; cook on
HIGH 3 hours.

2. Combine water, cornstarch, remaining ½ teaspoon curry powder and ½ teaspoon
ginger in small bowl; stir until cornstarch is dissolved. Add to pineapple mixture. Cook,
uncovered, on HIGH 15 minutes or until thickened.   *Makes 4½ cups*

Variation: Substitute 2 cans (20 ounces each) pineapple tidbits in heavy syrup for
pineapple and brown sugar.

1⅓ cups all-purpose flour

½ cup granulated sugar

1½ teaspoons baking powder

1½ teaspoons ground cinnamon

⅔ cup milk

5 tablespoons butter, melted, divided

1 cup chopped pecans

1½ cups water

¾ cup packed brown sugar

Whipped cream (optional)

1. Stir together flour, granulated sugar, baking powder and cinnamon in medium bowl.
Add milk and 3 tablespoons butter; mix just until blended. Stir in pecans. Spread on
bottom of slow cooker.

2. Combine water, brown sugar and remaining 2 tablespoons butter in small saucepan;
bring to a boil. Pour over batter in slow cooker.

3. Cover; cook on HIGH 1¼ to 1½ hours or until toothpick inserted into center comes
out clean. Let stand, uncovered, 30 minutes. Serve warm with whipped cream, if desired.
           Makes 8 servings

Prep Time: 20 minutes
Cook Time: 1¼ to 1½ hours (HIGH)
Stand Time: 30 minutes